THOUGHT

By Paul S. Osumi

From a Pacific Paradise Perspective

All rights reserved
Library of Congress Catalog Card
Number: 2002103836

ISBN 1-56647-549-X

Cover design by Sistenda Yim

First Printing, June 2002
1 2 3 4 5 6 7 8 9

Mutual Publishing
1215 Center Street, Suite 210
Honolulu, Hawai'i 96816
Ph: (808) 732-1709
Fax: (808) 734-4094
e-mail: mutual@lava.net
www.mutualpublishing.com

Printed in Australia

This booklet is dedicated
to the late
Dr. and Mrs. Theodore Richards
who promoted peace and goodwill
among the peoples of the
Pacific.

Preface

A woman wrote, "Could you not publish a little book of your 'Today's Thoughts'? I would run to the store the day it is offered for sale." Because of the many insistent requests such as this I have decided to publish this booklet of my little articles which have appeared in the HONOLULU ADVERTISER. I would feel amply rewarded if through these Thoughts even a few people could find a degree of spiritual strength and calm confidence in this bewildering age.

I wish to express my deep gratitude to the following people for assisting me in its publication: Mrs. Ah Jook Ku, Mrs. Frank E. Midkiff and J. M. Atherton Trust, Mr. Kum Pui Lai, Mr. Thurston Twigg-Smith, Mr. Howard Case, Mr. Robert Mattoch and my wife Janet. Thanks are due to all the readers of my column. Mahalo to all who have telephoned or written their encouragement to the author.

PAUL S. OSUMI

About The Author

Paul S. Osumi was minister of Nuuanu
Congregational Church in Honolulu. Two
years ago he served as president of the
Hawaiian Conference of the United Church
of Christ. He was one of the two corporate
members from Hawaii on the Board of
World Ministries of the United Church of
Christ. While a student at the University of
Hawaii he was a recipient of the Friend
Peace Scholarship. A graduate of the Uni-
versity of Southern California School of
Theology, he has served in churches in the
Islands and on the mainland. He was
chosen "Father of the Year in Religion" in
1963 by the Chamber of Commerce of
Honolulu. He is the author of the booklet,
"God in the Desert."

Contents

Aloha

"It is the unconditioned desire to promote the true good of other people in a friendly spirit out of a sense of kinship." This, according to a sermon by Dr. Abraham Akaka, minister of Kawaiahao Church, is the meaning of *aloha*. In our divided world, we desperately need *aloha*—a sense of kinship, coming from the belief that we all belong to only one race: the human race.

Live One Day

If you want to live without worry, live one day at a time. Drop yesterday with its mistakes and failures. Shut out tomorrow with its forebodings. Don't waste your time with futile fears and morbid musings. Each day is a little life. Be glad and grateful for its wonders. Live it with confidence and joy.

Two Tourists

"I am very disappointed in Hawaii," a tourist was heard to remark. "When I get back to the mainland, I will not have a good word about the islands." Another had this to say: "These are the friendliest isles. This is my second trip and I am determined that it shall not be my last." What we see depends on what we are.

Bad Luck

Lin Yutang, famous Chinese philosopher, says there is no bad luck because in the end the one balances the other. What looks like bad luck often turns out to be good, and good luck often means our downfall. Are you dogged by bad luck? Don't give up and lose your faith. Keep fighting. In the end you will come out the victor.

One's Age

A woman observing her birthday joyously proclaimed: "I am 71 years young; it's wonderful still to be so young." A young man left this suicide message: "Died of old age at 21." It is not how many years we live that really counts. It is how we live that truly matters. "Life is measured not by duration but by intensity."

The Moon

We talk nowadays about sending manned missiles to the moon, but we would do well to remember that our first responsibility is this world. Someone has aptly said: "Not great missiles to the moon but our mission to mankind must be our priority." Before we seek to conquer outer space, we must concentrate on conquering the evils of this world.

A Father Speaks

As a father tucked his child in bed, he reproached himself: "At breakfast I found fault. You spilled things, gulped down your food, spread butter too thick on your bread. I scolded you and nagged at you for almost everything. Forgive me for finding fault and reprimanding you for being a boy. I was measuring you by an adult yardstick."

Your Past Blunder

It is futile to torment yourself by brooding over past blunders. Too much self-reproach for things you cannot undo renders you unfit to do your best with what is left of life. Don't brood over past mistakes no matter how black they may be. Admit your faults and face the light.

Express Your Appreciation

A husband to his wife as he finished dinner: "Alice, that was the best chicken I have ever eaten." He always praised her culinary efforts. The art of expressing appreciation must be cultivated. No husband or wife should have to search far to find something to praise in the other. Learn to express your sincere appreciation.

Is God Dead?

One Sunday morning about church time a boy asked his father, "Daddy, is God dead?" Yes, God actually is dead in many a home. There is no prayer, no church, no grace at the table. Burdened with a thousand and one activities, many parents leave out the most important thing in life—the spiritual nurture of themselves and their children.

Spring In The Heart

Victor Hugo in his old age said, "Winter is on my head, but eternal spring is in my heart." If you have the spirit of youth with its courage, adventure, and enthusiasm, you are young. "Life begins at 40." You can start a better life at any age—40, 50, 60 or 80. "Life is measured, not by duration, but by intensity."

What Price Success?

Some people race along at top speed. They burn the candle at both ends. They neglect their rest, gulp down their food, and move fast in a wild dash to get ahead. Nothing stops them until a heart seizure forces them to lie motionless in a casket. What price success?

All Kinds Of People

While we live our short life on this earth, we come in contact with all kinds of people—people of various colors, shapes, sizes and ways of life. The problem is: What shall be the basis of our relationship with them? Some seek isolation. Some build a wall of prejudice. But life is deepest and richest when we seek to love and understand our neighbors.

A Sense Of Humor

Bennett Cerf, famous publisher-author-lecturer, exhorted a Honolulu audience: "Be happy. Go around with a grin and expect to have a good time and you'll have one. You get from life exactly what you put into it. We need a wholesome sense of humor." God pity us when we cease to smile or laugh at the lighter side of life.

Extras

"The joy of life is in its extras, the lovely things we do, the kind words we say, beyond what is expected of us." Yes, it is the unnecessary courtesies, the unexpected gifts, the uncalled-for thoughtfulness, and surprises of kindliness that make a happy home.

Nagging

If you want to make your home an unhappy place, nag. If you want to drive your husband or wife away from you, nag. If you want your child's behavior to get worse, nag. If you want to alienate the affection of your loved one, nag. Nagging creates an atmosphere of confusion and conflict in which love suffocates.

Sail On

On the day his crew threatened mutiny and the storm damaged his ships, Columbus wrote in his diary five words, "This day we sailed on." The ocean of life is not always calm. The real test comes when life brings us a bitter experience, a sad disappointment, or a heart-breaking failure. Let us determine to sail on.

True Success

We often think of success in terms of money one has accumulated or fame one has attained. But here is a definition of true success: "He has achieved success who has lived well, laughed often, and loved much; who has filled his niche and accomplished his task; who has always looked for the best in others, and given the best he had."

Humanity Is One

Confucianism teaches: "All within the four seas are brothers." For Buddhism, "There is no caste in blood, which runneth of one hue." Christianity holds that "God hath made of one blood all nations of men for to dwell on the face of the earth." Yes, people are people everywhere. They have the same basic drives—the same hopes, fears, and aspirations.

Boredom

We spend our days doing routine work. We sit before the same desk in the same office to put down columns of figures or pound a typewriter day in and day out. To bear the monotonous burdens of our daily life and not be overcome with boredom and futility—that is victorious living.

Wrinkles In The Heart

A speaker warned his audience, "Have a care lest the wrinkles in the face extend to the heart." It is not shameful to have wrinkles in the face. But it is tragic to have wrinkles in the heart. Some people allow the cares of life to make them sour, ill-tempered, complaining. Avoid the wrinkles inside of you.

Money, Money, Money

"Oh, money, money, money, thou art health and life and peace; he that hath thee can rattle his pockets at the devil." Can he? Can he rattle his pockets at unhappiness, at sickness, at death? All the money in the world cannot buy one's health. All the money in the world cannot buy inner peace and happiness.

What Is Life?

"Life today is a hideous humdrum, a ghastly joke. Birth, toil, death and, at the · end, a jump in the dark— nothing else." On the contrary, life is largely what we make of it. Life can be an exciting adventure, an abundant joy. Friendship, laughter, beauty, love, and, at the end, an open door— and eternal life.

Faith In Humanity

Every year the men of the 27th Wolfhound Infantry at Schofield Barracks, Hawaii, invite a little girl from a Japanese orphanage in Osaka, Japan, as their special guest of honor. These men have been contributing a sum each month to help support the orphanage. Deeds such as this warm our hearts and renew our faith in humanity and democracy.

Mud Or Stars

"Two men looked out of the prison bars. One saw mud and the other stars." Life can be mud or stars depending on your outlook. If you have eyes only for criticism you can always find fault in everything and everybody. On the other hand, if you have eyes of appreciation, lo, the whole world changes into one of beauty and loveliness.

An Understanding Parent

A parent's prayer: "O God, teach me to understand my children, to listen to them patiently, and to answer all their questions honestly. Let me never nag; and when I am out of sorts, help me to hold my tongue. Let me praise them for all deserving deeds. May I encourage them to think, to choose, and to make decisions. Make me an understanding parent."

Keeping Up With The Joneses

Many people lie awake at night worrying about how to make both ends meet. Rising prices and soaring taxes harass and annoy them. They try to stretch an income to obtain innumerable things they want. Stop keeping up with the Joneses. Learn to go without some luxuries. This is one way to live without worry.

Handicap

Do you have some handicap? Are you having a hard time? Stop pitying yourself. Accept your hand as it was dealt to you and play the game. Don't waste your time bemoaning the fact that your cards are not all aces. Accept yourself for what you are, and for what, by the grace of God, you may yet become, and play the game.

Do It Now

If you intend to speak a kind word, speak it now. If you intend to do a kind deed, do it now. If you intend to write a letter to your friend, write it today. If you intend to send flowers to your loved one, send them today. Tomorrow may be too late. You may not be here tomorrow. Your friend may not be here tomorrow.

In The Mind

Many of our illnesses have their origin in the mind. Our disturbing sense of guilt and our deep-seated fear play havoc with our health. Our grudges, resentments, envy, and jealousy poison our body and destroy our physical health. A physician said, "Ninety per cent of my patients would be well, if they found God."

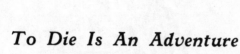

To Die Is An Adventure

Sir James M. Barrie said, "To die will be an awfully big adventure." Life after death cannot be proved. But that ought not to disturb us. The things we can prove in life do not make life exciting. The most thrilling things are the uncertainties. Trust in God and do not fear death.

Only Skin Deep

"Unhappiness Is Only Skin Deep" headlined an advertisement on a new book on plastic surgery. The sad fact is that many people believe happiness comes from superficial things. Happiness cannot be obtained through external means and satisfaction of our physical desires. It is primarily a spiritual matter. It comes from within.

Father Was Too Busy

A father whose son had gotten into trouble pondered, "I can't understand. We have treated him well. He had his own room, his own camera, and his own gun. He had everything." Yes, he had everything except his father's time and interest. The father was too busy to give his son a part of himself.

A High Opinion Of Himself

A man was asked why he talked to himself so much. He replied, "For two reasons. First, I like to talk to a smart man. Second, I like to hear a smart man talk." This man had a high opinion of himself. There is something sacred in each one of us. Let us "be loyal to the royal" in ourselves.

"I Haven't Given Up Hope"

Florence Mizuuchi, 20, was walking in a pedestrians' crosswalk when she became the victim of a serious automobile accident. One of the cars struck her from the back, pinned her against a telephone pole and injured both her legs. Her right one had to be amputated. With tears in her eyes but courage in her heart, her brave comment: "I haven't given up hope!"

Deadly Weapons

A food chemist once observed, "The deadly weapons used by man in committing suicide are the knife, fork and spoon." We must keep our bodies fit by taking proper food, rest, exercise and sunshine. We must watch our weight. It is just as religious for us to observe the rules of good health as to pray to God to heal our sick bodies.

A Dagger

"If fate throws a dagger at you, there are two places to take hold of it—by the blade or by the handle." If fate throws a misfortune at you, you can take it by the blade of self-pity and it will cut and hurt you. If you take it by the handle, you can use it and turn it into a fortune.

The Sure Cure

High blood pressure, nervous breakdowns, ulcers and mental collapses are often caused, our doctors tell us, by negative thinking, evil imagination and confused emotions. It is hard to cure them with pills, injections or surgery. The sure cure is the practice of love and forgiveness.

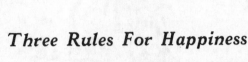

Three Rules For Happiness

Alice Freeman Palmer advocates three simple rules for happiness. First, commit to memory every day something good, such as a Bible verse. Second, look for something pretty each day—a flower, a cloud, a star, and stop long enough before it to say, "Isn't it beautiful?" Third, do something for someone every day.

The Aspirin Age

Someone has characterized this as "The Aspirin Age." Living a fast, hectic, worry-laden life, we often develop headaches. To cure these headaches we consume aspirin. It is said that 4 million pounds of aspirin are consumed each year in the United States. The need of the hour is faith —faith in God who gives us real peace of mind.

The Meaning Of Life

What is the meaning of our short life on this earth? If we have learned to live without fear, to drop our hate and bitterness toward others, to go through our pain and suffering without complaint, to see beauty in common things around us, to be glad to be alive and unafraid to die, then we are achieving the goals of life.

Right Where You Are

The most exciting and interesting place is right where you are. If the grass is greener in your neighbor's backyard, it usually is because he has made it greener. Stop envying others. You can make your life happier and better by changing your attitude. Do the best with what you have right where you are.

Worry

"Worry is like a rocking chair—it will give you something to do but won't get you anywhere." Not only that—it will wear you out getting nowhere. But you need not live a strained life. Commit your fears into God's hands. Let go of your tensions and let God take hold of your life.

Stunted Trees

The Japanese very cleverly stunt great forest trees and make them into potted plants by tying up the taproot. The trees then live off their surface roots only, and their growth is stunted. Many people are tied up with fears, guilts, resentments, inferiority complexes and self-centered thoughts. Only God can release them.

Be Kind

Ian MacLaren, the Scottish writer said, "Let us be kind to one another, for most of us are fighting a hard battle." An outward appearance is often deceiving. A man may be smiling, but in his heart he may be nursing a deep hurt. A man, joking with his friends, may be hiding deep anguish in his soul. It always pays to be kind.

Set Your Aims High

Henry J. Kaiser, famous industrialist and developer of Hawaii-Kai, subscribes to this basic creed: "Your plan for work and happiness should be big, imaginative, and daring." Human beings are meant for struggle and for climbing. We must dream, aspire and set our aims high. We become better and happier when we are strongly held by some high ambition.

Married Happiness

The prize winners at a picnic were announced, "Mrs. Smith won the ladies' rolling pin-throwing contest. Mr. Smith won the 100-yard dash." The art of being happy, though married, is difficult to master. Friction is bound to rise between husband and wife, but it must be resolved in love and not in a loss of temper.

The Added Touch

The secret of success in any undertaking is the added touch—doing more than is expected. The store that gives the added service, the restaurant that serves the extra cup, the gasoline station that gives its customers superior service, the hotel that places a newspaper at each door in the morning—these have learned the secret of winning favor and business.

Later Than You Think

A bronze tablet on a wall in a Chinese garden contained these words, "Enjoy yourself. It is later than you think." If you are planning to do better tomorrow, you had better not wait. Tomorrow may never come. You had better begin today. To many people a better future never comes because they neglect what they ought to do today.

Fighting The Problem

A certain teacher repeatedly admonishes his class, "Don't fight the problem." What he means is that the energy spent in worrying about the problem should be spent in finding its solution. Are you faced with a problem? Are you brooding over it? Why not begin doing something constructive in solving it?

Stop Imagining Things

We often make ourselves miserable worrying about something that never happens. We make ourselves unhappy anticipating trouble that never comes. We spend agonizing hours expecting a malady from which we will never suffer. We lose sleep weeping over sorrows that never arrive. The best advice is, "Stop imagining things."

To Live Is To Suffer

To live is to suffer in many ways. We can never change that fact. But the decisive thing is not the event itself but our reaction in the face of of it. There is no misfortune, no defeat, no burden of sorrow or suffering so great that a person, with God's help, cannot rise above it.

Human Beings

A child heard the term "human beings" but could not grasp its meaning. His mother explained, "It means all of us—father, mother, brother, sister, our neighbors; everyone we know is a human being." The child asked, "But all the people we don't know, are they human beings?" Ah, there's the rub. All the people we don't know, are they human beings too? Do we treat them as our brothers?

Feeling Trapped

Two skeletons were hanging in a closet. One said, "You know, if we had any guts, we'd get out of here." Some people feel trapped in life. Bitter and frustrated with their lot they come to feel that life itself has no meaning. But men of faith can always see a way out and begin to live a new life.

Only One Problem

In these days of pressure and tension, we are driven almost to distraction by our work. How many times have you thought as you went to bed, "How can I ever meet all the tasks of tomorrow?" But you must remember that in a given instant of time only one difficulty can possibly emerge to perplex you. You have to handle only one problem at a time.

In The Garden

A bit of wisdom from an old Indian book: "Dig a big hole in the garden of your thoughts. Into it put all your disillusions, disappointments, regrets, worries, troubles, doubts and fears—and forget. Cover well with the earth of fruitfulness. Sow on top the seeds of hope, courage, strength, patience and love. Water it from the well of content."

Light A Candle

The Christophers teach that it is better to light a candle than curse the darkness. They stress the importance of the individual in the righting of wrong. At times you feel you are alone and helpless, but if you do your duty and bear your witness, then together with thousands of others, you can make your influence felt for good.

Life Is An Adventure

It is good to see a man who loves life, who enjoys it and does not simply endure it. It is good to see a man to whom life is an adventure, not a burden. The secret of his joy in living is that he is not imprisoned within himself. He has learned to enjoy and live with others.

"Blue" Days

Every person will find that he sometimes has dark days—days when he feels he is "down in the dumps." So do thousands of people. But we do well to remember that "blue" days do pass. We must not let them upset us and crush us. We must accept them, look upon them as passing clouds, and wait until the sun shines—as it surely will.

Parental Delinquency

Honolulu Police Chief Dan Liu's candid observation: "Our problem is not so much one of juvenile delinquency as it is of parental delinquency." Actually there is no juvenile problem. It is always an adult problem. Children copy what we do. What we do speak more loudly than what we tell our children to do. "Age needs critics but youth needs models."

A Number Of Things

Stevenson wrote, "The world is so
full of a number of things I'm sure we
should be as happy as kings." Today
our world has many more things than
in Stevenson's day. We push buttons
and we have light, music, heat and
even movies. But has not the increase
of things multiplied our confusion?
Has it not robbed us of life's deepest
meaning?

The Same Dishes

A woman complained she washed the same dishes every day. If they all were stacked up, they would be higher than the Washington Monument. Yes, life is often colorless, deadly and monotonous. Every day we get up, eat, go to work, then come home and go to bed again. But life is what we make it. It depends on our attitude. Cheer up, friends. Pull yourselves together.

One World

The late Wendell Wilkie coined the phrase, "One world." Yes, we live in one world. We all live under one roof. What happens in one part of the world affects the rest of it. We must show our concern for people everywhere. Only as we develop for one another a sense of oneness can there come an abiding peace.

Frustration

Everywhere we meet men and women who are frustrated. To overcome the feeling of frustration we must accept facts about ourselves. One woman admitted, "The happiest day of my life was the day I gave up trying to be beautiful." There are some things you cannot do no matter how hard you try. To be happy, accept and be yourself.

Live Upstairs

Ernest Dimnet in his book, "What We Live By," says that we have an upstairs and a downstairs in our life. To live a radiant life we must consciously try to live in the upstairs plane. That means that we must read good books, listen to lovely music, associate with stimulating friends, think noble thoughts and do kind deeds.

Poverty

Poverty is not always a matter of economics. A man living in an exclusive neighborhood with a station wagon and a sport car in his garage can be poor. On the other hand, a man living in a shack with nothing on the floor can be rich. Poor is he who has no friends. Poor is he who has no dream. Poor indeed is he who has no faith in God.

How To Win Friends

A young woman asked her marital adviser how she could induce a certain young man to propose to her. The adviser replied, "The best way to get a husband is to talk to a man about himself." If you want to win friends, forget yourself, and learn to love and be interested in other people. Practice the Golden Rule.

Graying Hair

William Lyon Phelps once gave this advice on the subject of graying hair, "Were your hair to turn green or blue, then surely you ought to see a doctor! But when it turns gray, as nature intended, wear it proudly like a flag. You are fortunate in a world of so many vicissitudes to have lived long enough to earn it."

A Long Headache

Masefield is credited with this line: "Life's a long headache in a noisy street." We often get caught up in the incidentals of daily existence and lose sight of the meaning of life. Life gets to be "full of sound and fury, signifying nothing." To recover life's meaning, we would do well to spend a few minutes each day to think and meditate and pray.

When You Retire

Some people say, "I will work extra hard so I can retire early with enough money to play and have a good time." But the trouble is that when you do retire you may not know how to have a good time, or you may be too old to pursue your interests. If you intend to take music lessons, or paint pictures or read good books, start now.

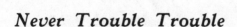

Never Trouble Trouble

There was a woman who for 50 years had the habit of looking under her bed every night for a burglar. If she had found one she probably would have died of shock. Many people worry about things that never happen. Someone wisely said, "Better never trouble trouble until trouble troubles you."

The Way To Love

"The way to love anything is to realize that it might be lost." As we meditate over it we will come to see its truth. A good way to love the members of our family is by remembering that they might be lost. A good way to love our country is by realizing that its blessings might be lost.

A *Second Choice*

In life we cannot always realize our
ambition. Our plan is often upset and
our dream shattered. Few men are
now doing what they first wanted to
do. It takes courage to take a broken
plan and make a great thing of it.
Don't hold a grudge against life if
you can't have your own way. Take
a second choice and make the best
of it.

A Thorn In The Flesh

To have to face life with a handicap, a constant thorn in the flesh, a cranky boss, a nagging wife, a thoughtless husband, an invalid to care for, a monotonous job—that is being sentenced to live. And when these are met faithfully and borne cheerfully, not as a drudgery, not with complaint, therein lies the victory of life.

A Barrel Of Gold

A kindly happy man once was asked why he acted as though he didn't have a care in the world. He replied, "Because I have a barrel of gold at home." Some thieves broke into his home to steal his barrel of gold. He did have a barrel of gold at home, but no one could steal it. His barrel of gold was the love he had for his family, and the love his family had for him.

"Smothered" By Scenery

A few years ago a Chinese play, "The White Snake Lady," was staged in Honolulu. There was hardly any scenery but the lack of it was more than offset by the beautiful costumes and brilliant acting. Some plays are "smothered" by scenery. In life one's possessions and pleasures tend to smother his soul.

Never Say Die

A passenger was terribly seasick on the ship deck. A steward came along and said, "Cheer up, sir. No man ever died of seasickness." The sick man replied, "Please don't say that. It's the hope of dying that has kept me alive so far." No matter how discouraging a situation you may be in, never give up hope. Where there is life there is hope.

A Necessary Evil

Many persons do not succeed in their work because they look upon it as something to be endured, not enjoyed; a necessary evil, not an opportunity for growth and self-expression. We should all examine ourselves to see whether we have this attitude, and do all we can to eliminate it if we wish to get ahead.

Be Yourself

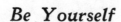

Clark Gable, in the movie, "It Happened One Night", took off his shirt and displayed no undershirt. Subsequently, men's underwear showed a 40 percent drop in sales in a single year. It is a pity people copy what others do. They think, talk, vote and live in accordance with the social pattern. We need courage to be our own individual selves.

Each Day Is A Little Life

Dr. Joseph Newton points out that each day is a little life and each night a tiny death when we are lost in sleep. Yesterday is gone. Tomorrow is not yet here. Today is all we have. So let us not worry about yesterday or tomorrow. Let us live today as we know we should—strongly, bravely, cheerfully, helpfully.

Better People

The improvement of our society depends not so much on social reform as on spiritual regeneration. "The heart of reform is really the reform of the heart." What the world really needs is not better roads, better plumbing, better cars or better theaters, but better people. We need: not mechanization of life but spiritualization of life.

The Foolish Man

The foolish man is one who works without rest. He goes to the office Saturdays, Sundays, and holidays. He never wastes time in recreation. He always eats in a hurry. He never reads a book, never takes time to play with his children, never takes a vacation, and never visits with friends. And he goes to his grave sooner than his time.

Induced By Drugs

The *New Yorker* carried this cartoon: Two young women, in a small apartment, are trying to relax after returning from their day's work. One says to the other, "I don't know whether to take a Benzedrine and go to the party or a Nembutal and go to bed." Many people live such an empty life that their gaiety and sleep must be induced by drugs.

Our Turn

Almost every day we read of the death of someone we know. We are prompted to reflect, "Will my life be similarly cut short?" We all tend to think we have plenty of time and there is no hurry. But often "it is later than we think." We must do all the good we can before our turn comes.

"I And Thou"

When the body of Dag Hammarskjold, Secretary General of the United Nations, was found in a plane wreck, he had with him the book, "I And Thou" by Martin Buber—a book expounding a philosophy which Hammarksjold felt was the last hope of humanity. The author's thesis is this: Our relationship with others must be one of sharing, understanding and love.

Charity Begins At Home

Edward Howe said, "Instead of trying to love your enemies, treat your friends a little better." The trouble with us is that we find it difficult to care for the people closest to us. We have not learned to love the very people about whom we know the most. Charity begins at home. Let us be kind and affectionate ever mindful of our family and friends.

Backache Now

After working all day a man was seen playing baseball with his son. The friend, looking over the fence, queried him, "Bill, aren't you tired?" The man replied, "Why, yes, I am." Friend: "Well, what under the sun are you doing that for?" Response: "I'd rather have the backache now than the heartache later."

Zest Of Living

The tragedy of life is that often its freshness fades. The work which we begin with high hopes and interest degenerates into dreary monotony. The marriage, begun with such bliss, becomes commonplace. The ambitions that once stirred us becomes lifeless. The saddest thing that can happen to anyone is to lose the thrill and zest of living.

A Curse Of Humanity

There was a woman who hated people of a certain race. Asked why she hated them, she could not give any good reason. Yet this woman was kindhearted—putting out bread for the birds every day. Racial prejudice is blind and bigoted. It prejudges and condemns people before the evidence is heard. It is a curse of humanity.

Identification

In introducing a speaker at a banquet once, the toastmaster had this to say about him: "This man has been closely identified with all the good things in our community for more than 50 years." Identified with all the good things — what a tribute! A man's life is measured — not by his possessions — but by things with which he has been associated and identified.

Living Negatively

Today there are millions of people trying to live in a negative manner. They are against this and that but they have no positive values of their own. It is easier to criticize someone else than to do something constructively ourselves. It is easier to attack the allegiances of others than to have some allegiance ourselves.

An Optimist

"An optimist is like a tea kettle that manages to whistle even though it is up to its neck in hot water." An optimist in actual life: A soldier who had lost both arms and legs in war yet was grateful because "I still have my health and strength left." He has something else besides—his indomitable spirit. In the struggle called life, we all need to be optimists.

Risking Your Life

A few years ago Devere Baker, with a crew of three, succeeded in landing on the island of Maui after having drifted 69 days on a raft from California. He was trying to prove the theory that Hawaii was settled by men drifting from the Americas. Are you willing to risk your life to prove what you believe?

Crumbs Of Happiness

Happiness eludes us because we look for it from afar. We need to learn that joy comes from an appreciation of the simple things. "A quiet hour in the sun, a few pages of a book, a flash of sunset, a beautiful flower, a passing smile, a kindly word, a little gift—these are the crumbs of happiness."

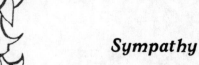

Sympathy

A man saw a number of children on a street, all crying. He asked them, "What's the matter with you children?" They answered, "We've all got a pain in Billy's stomach." Real sympathy is not simply feeling sorry for the misfortune of another. It is putting oneself in another's place. It is making somebody else's pain your own.

Go To Church

Someone jokingly remarked, "Whenever I go past a church, I always stop to visit, so that when at last I'm carried in, the Lord won't say, 'Who is it?' ". In order to maintain our spiritual health, church going is a necessity. In these days of uncertainty, we need the certainty that comes from our faith in God. Go to church.

"Show Me"

In the play, "My Fair Lady," a suitor glowingly declares his love for Eliza, the heroine. Eliza responded, "Show me!" It is one thing to declare one's love for someone. But it is another thing to demonstrate that love. Actions speak louder than words. Demonstration is always better than declaration.

Live Dangerously

To the late President John Kennedy "This is a dangerous and uncertain world. No one expects our lives to be easy—not in this decade, not in this century." Danger is an integral part of human life. Anything that is worthwhile is apt to be dangerous. To live a meaningful life we must not play it safe. We must live dangerously.

Giving Is Receiving

A prosperous manufacturer donated to a church a pipe organ costing $25,000. Then the depression came and his business collapsed. Today he is on the caretaker's staff of the church to which he gave the organ. To a recent visitor he revealed his philosophy, "That which I kept I lost, and that which I gave, I still have."

Sex Attraction

Many a young man marries a girl for her beautiful face or her attractive figure. Many a girl marries a man for his handsome looks. But the trouble is that physical attraction doesn't last long. The time will come when he starts to bulge in the middle and she will start to sag in the wrong places. The romance built only on sex attraction is often doomed to failure.

Follow Your Rainbow

The Mother Superior in Rodgers and Hammerstein's "The Sound of Music" sings this piece of advice to the girl who had left the convent because of her love for a man: "Climb ev'ry mountain, ford ev'ry stream, follow ev'ry rainbow, till you find your dream!" Life becomes zestful when you start on your adventurous trip to realize your dream.

Worshipping "Bigness"

Here in America we tend to worship bigness. We are impressed by what is big—big cities, big buildings, big corporations. But size is an utterly fallacious standard when we are trying to estimate power. Bigness is not power. Power is in creative ideas and ideals that uphold society.

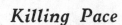

Killing Pace

The president of a bank dropped the telephone receiver back into its cradle and said to his secretary. "They have just found John dead at his desk —a heart attack!" Every morning's paper tells of someone dying of a heart attack or a stroke. Modern life drives people to live at a killing pace. Why not slow down and live longer?

Why Not A Perfect World?

An atheist cynically asked, "Why didn't God, if there is one, make a perfect world?" But suppose we lived in a world where there were no bridges to build, no oceans to cross, no cities to plan, no food to raise, no mountains to climb; what an uninteresting world it would be. There is no challenge in the perfect.

How To Die

A group of soldiers was being entertained before leaving for the war front. One of them asked, "Will any of our friends here tell us how to die?" There was a silence. Then one of the singers began to sing the aria from "Elijah"—"O Rest in the Lord." If we have a firm faith in God, we can face death without fear.

Four Essentials

Dr. Richard Cabot in his book, "What Men Live By," says that we need four things to make our life complete: Work, play, love and worship. Yes, it is true that "all work and no play makes Jack a dull boy." Without love life is empty. We desperately need to worship God who is greater and wiser than our little selves.

Twenty-One Words

When Dr. William Osler was a young man, he picked up a book and read twenty-one words that had a profound effect upon his future. The words which helped him lead a life free from worry were from Thomas Carlyle, "Our main business in life is not to see what lies dimly at a distance, but to do what lies ahead clearly at hand."

No Time To Live

A man wrote his own epitaph: "Born a human being. Died a whole-sale grocer." He explained, "I was so busy selling groceries that I had no time for my family and friends. I was so busy making money that I had no time for lectures, concerts, books, church and community service. I was so busy making a living that I never had time to live."

Brotherhood

We often talk glibly about "building bridges of understanding" around the world. However, brotherhood ought to begin at home on a person-to-person basis. We must cultivate friendships with persons of other races in our country, in our state, in our city, in our neighborhood, in our housing, in our schools, in our clubs, in our jobs, in our shop or office.

The Ocean Of Life

Not long ago Florentino Daz, an adventurous Filipino young man, got in a small boat in Kewalo Basin in Honolulu, and ventured out on a long and perilous solo trip to the Philippines. Many laughed at his recklessness. But with dauntless courage and uncanny skill, he made it. The ocean of life is wide and tumultous at times, but we too can make it, if we have God as our Pilot.

Each Today

Kazuo Kage of Wailuku, Maui, said, "Live each today so that when each tomorrow comes, each today will be a pleasant yesterday." This is a good philosophy. Don't burden yourself with the regrets of yesterday and fears of tomorrow. Live each day the best you know how. Live each day as if it were the only day you had. Live each day as if there were no tomorrow.

Be A Forgetter

Sometime ago a memory expert came to Honolulu to show people how to improve their memory. It is advantageous for us to have a good memory. But it is more important to be a good forgetter, provided we forget the right things. We do well to forget yesterday's neglects, failures, disappointments, sorrows, insults and grudges.

The Grumbling Habit

The worst habit to fall into is the grumbling habit. It can spoil the whole climate of one's life. To a grumbler nothing is right and something is the matter with everything. He sees only the gloomy side of life. A person who is occupied with complaints seldom thinks about the needs of others. He is constantly unhappy and dissatisfied.

Immature Adults

It is a tragedy that many adults are immature. The man who "blows his top" when breakfast is not ready when he happens to be ready is immature. The wife who works up a domestic crisis over a trifle has not grown up. The woman who becomes upset when her name has been omitted from the list of committee members shows her immaturity. Emotional growth is just as important as physical growth.

The Art Of
Sitting Quietly

In her book, "Gift from the Sea," Anne Lindbergh tells how she goes apart from the world to a quiet beach where she can be by herself. If you can't go to a quiet place, why not go into your room for 15 minutes a day, close the door, turn off the radio or television, take the telephone off the hook, and sit and meditate and pray?

Stick Your Neck Out

A man had on his desk a model of a turtle under which were these words, "Consider the turtle. He makes progress only when he sticks his neck out." When a turtle is enclosed in his shell he makes no progress. Are you afraid to take any risks for a good cause? Are you afraid to stick your neck out to help your fellow men?

Lost Enthusiasm

A school teacher wrote a minister, "I have been teaching for a number of years and long ago all the newness wore off my work. Some days it seems I cannot continue teaching another minute. And this is followed by a mood of complete indifference to my work." He was speaking for many people in all walks of life. We desperately need to regain enthusiasm in our work and life.

Enriching Our Minds

A cartoon showed a man looking out of a library window, saying, "What on earth can a man do on a rainy day like this?" The question is absurd. Here is a man in a room full of books, and not knowing how to spend his time. Reading good books is one of the best ways to enrich our minds.

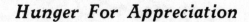

Hunger For Appreciation

We all hunger for appreciation. We all crave the words of approval and recognition that make our efforts seem worthwhile. It is tragic that many people keep on with their task, day in and day out, week in week out, and hardly anybody ever utters a word of praise for their efforts. Interest and encouragement are essential to life.

Keep Your Chin Up

Life is hard for many of us and cruel for some of us. We all need to keep our chin up. We must not let life get us down, trample and crush us. We must rebuke our fears, rally our faith, and renew our fighting spirit. We must not bend under the pressure of trouble. No matter what happens, refuse to surrender. Always keep your chin up!

One At A Time

A tired man asks, "When can I ever get through today? Look at all the things I must do." In a single instant of time only one thing can emerge to perplex us. We must learn to live one moment at a time, face one difficulty at a time, and carry one burden at a time. Then we can accomplish much with ease.

Superstitions

"I haven't had a cold for months—knock on wood." How many conversations are prefaced by the phrase, "Knock on wood"! In this scientific age many people succumb to unreasonable fears and superstitions. They have mental reservations about the power of black cats, stepladders, rabbits' feet and good luck symbols. We do well to rid ourselves of all superstitious beliefs.

What A Cast!

A playwright, looking up a number in a New York City telephone directory, commented, "Not much plot here but what a cast!" In the Honolulu telephone directory we find long lists of Yamamotos, Tanakas, Lees, Chings, Smiths, Fernandezes, and Ramoses. All religions, races and colors! Yes, Hawaii can play a great drama on the world's stage.

A Good Digestion

"Give me a good digestion, Lord, and also something to digest; Give me a healthy body, Lord, with a sense to keep it at its best; Give me a mind that is not bored, that does not whimper, whine, nor sigh; Give me a sense of humor, Lord, Give me the grace to see a joke, to get some pleasure out of life and pass it on to other folk."

Minor Parts

Among items in a metropolitan newspaper was this brief comment on the death of an actor, "He played minor parts like a master." Our lives are made up of minor parts—dish washing, writing letters, answering door bells, working in the office, etc. Pray not for great deeds but pray, rather, for willingness to do little things in a great way.

Being Neutral

A man described how he avoided getting involved in squabbles, "I just put myself in neutral and take it easy." The trouble with the world is that too many people have put themselves in neutral. They take no part in the struggle of right against evil. We must not be neutral in battles for civic decency, human rights, brotherhood and peace.

Life's Needs

Emerson said the needs of life are much fewer than most people realize. We need someone to love and be loved so that we can share our sorrows and our joys. We need something worth doing so that we can fill time and not kill it. We need faith in God that makes sense out of life.

Fools

A minister announced, "Next Sunday my sermon topic will be 'Fools', and I hope a great many will attend." It is hard for anyone to be called a fool and become a victim of ridicule. Often a man with an ideal is called a dreamer, crank, or fanatic. Never mind the jibes and derision of others. Stand for your convictions and do what is right.

When God Is Silent

On the walls of a cellar in Cologne, Germany, where a number of escaped prisoners of war hid out during the last War, there was found this inscription, "I believe in the sun, even when it is not shining. I believe in love, even when feeling it not. I believe in God, even when He is silent."

Enlarging Our Circle

An old man used to repeat this prayer every day, "Lord, bless me and my wife, my son John and his wife, us four and no more." Some people are so self-centered that they don't care a bit about other people. We must broaden our outlook and include in our circle of concern other people. We must assume our responsibility for our fellow human beings.

Real Education

Some people have the erroneous idea that education is cramming the mind of the child with facts and information. That is not so. The word "education" comes from the Latin verb "educare" which means to draw out. Real education is drawing out the best in the child by the persuasive appeal of the teacher.

Defects In Human Relationships

A business executive said, "I think that more people fail because of defects in human relationships than for any other reason." Here is a young man with ability and education who is constantly changing his job and never forges ahead. He has not learned to get along with people. To succeed in life, take an active interest in other people. Put yourself in the place of others.

Only Once

The sudden death of a friend makes us realize that our life on this earth is short. We do well to think of the words of Phillips Brooks, "I expect to pass through this world but once; any good therefore that I can do, or any kindness I can show to any fellow creature, let me do it now. Let me not defer or neglect it, for I shall not pass this way again."

Life's Prisons

"Stone walls do not prison make, nor iron bars a cage." All of the people who are in prison are not behind bars. Many are victims of prison houses which they have built for themselves. Often they become captives of their own lusts, their own hates, their own resentments, their own impulses. We do well to ask God to free us from our life's prisons.

Drudgery Or Joy

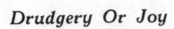

Time magazine once said of Willie May, the great player with the San Francisco Giants, "Willie plays baseball with a boy's glee, a pro's sureness, and a champion's flair." Whether one's work becomes drudgery or joy depends on his attitude toward it. To derive pleasure from work, one must approach it with enthusiasm and seek to improve his skill and efficiency.

Walls And Bridges

Father Dominique Pire, a recipient of the Nobel Prize for Peace, believes, "Men build too many walls and not enough bridges." We build a wall and shut out from our association those whose ideas we disagree. We build a wall against those who have slighted us. Why not build bridges of understanding, reconciliation, sympathy and love?

He Died Climbing

In the Alps there is a monument erected to the memory of a man who lost his life seeking to ascend the mountain. The stone bears this simple inscription, "He died climbing." The three words recite his life of heroism. He did not reach the summit, but he fell with his face toward it. In spite of the struggle, we must go forward.

Meaningless Activity

A cartoon showed a husband and wife driving along at rapid pace on a desert road. The wife: "I know we're lost, but I didn't want to say anything about it because we were making such good time." There are many people who keep themselves busy—and ,yet do nothing. The tragedy of life is meaningless activity without objective.

How To Combat Communism

Communism can not be combatted by attacking it only with invectives. The better way to meet it is by giving the people a better way of life. The unfair treatment of minorities and the inequalities and injustices of society play right into the hands of Communists. We must give every person a degree of human dignity and a reasonable opportunity to lead a good life.

The Sound Of Music

Shakespeare said, "The man who hath not music in his soul, who is not moved by concord of sweet sounds, is fit for treason's stratagems, and spoils. Let no such man be trusted." Every human being should enjoy music. Music is a universal language which speaks its joy, its sadness or its challenge to all people everywhere.

Joining Our Hands

Once a little child was lost in a wheatfield. His parents searched in vain to find the child. The neighbors and friends came to assist in the search. They couldn't find the child. Then someone suggested, "Why don't we join our hands and comb the entire field?" So they did. They found the child—dead. They said, "Why didn't we join our hands sooner?"

Forgiving Ourselves

It is hard to forgive others. It is harder still to forgive oneself. How can we forgive ourselves for something we have done, or left undone? Futile remorse and a sense of guilt can wreck a human life, paralyzing the very soul, if not the body. If we are to be healthy in body and mind, we must forgive ourselves.

Three More Years To Live

A man was told by his doctor that he had only three more years to live. Instead of brooding over his misfortune, he decided to spend the remaining three years of his life as best as he could. He read great books, listened to great music, visited orphanages and hospitals, and did all he could for others. Just before he died, he said, "I have no regrets. I am ready to go."

God's Telephone Number

A preacher said, "The trouble is that we want to ring God up on the phone, but we don't know His number." Petty, selfish prayers will not reach God. If we have hate in our hearts, our prayers will die on our lips. God is known only through love. Love is the number. No other number will reach Him.

To Live Is To Give

William Blake wrote, "He who gives when he is asked has waited too long." Some give under constraint. Some give because they are expected to. Some give because they feel they ought to. But they all miss the joy of true giving—giving voluntarily and sacrificially. To make the most of life you must give it away. "To live is to give."

Criticism

In life we are bound to be misunderstood and criticized by others. Especially if you occupy a position of prominence you will certainly become the target of misunderstandings and abuses. Washington was called a hypocrite. Lincoln was described as the original gorilla. Don't be upset by criticism. Do what is right in the sight of God and fear no one.

Whistle A Tune

When the mother of our former Governor William F. Quinn was asked what she remembered about the boyhood of her famous son, she said, "He was a normal, happy boy. He always had a song in his heart and on his lips." When you are downhearted, why not whistle the tune of a happy song? When things look gloomy and dark, why not sing a song of praise to God?

A Guide For Life

"Talk with God before you talk with man; do your daily work with sunshine in your face; be energetic but not fussy; be true to yourself, and false to no man; be loyal to principle at the cost of popularity; humor no one simply because he is rich; despise no man simply because he is poor; and leave the world a better for your stay."

Little Surprises

A man was asked for the secret of his happy home life. He answered, "Little surprises." He went on to explain that once a week he would pick up a little surprise for his wife on his way home. His child might surprise him by shining his shoes without his knowledge. His wife would slip a cute magazine clipping on his desk.

You Can't Take It With You

There is a famous play entitled, "You Can't Take It With You." It is foolish to devote all of our time and effort in accumulating money and things which we can't take with us when we die. But we can give ourselves to others. We can work for God. We can go out of this world with our hands laden with good deeds.